Welcome to *Book 8*. In this book you will
words, and both Nicola and Jem will int
exciting word study activities.

Hi! I'm Jem.

Hello! I'm Nicola. Jem and I work hard at spelling but our favourite activity is making music.

I'm Mr D – the teacher. You probably met me in Book 7. Like Nicola and Jem I also like making music – but I know which activities are really important in life.

Let's check the way we learn to spell a word.

1 Find the **hardspot** – that part of the word that gives you trouble.
2 Close your eyes. Try to imagine that you can see the word.
3 Say the letters in order as you would say a phone number.
4 Write the word once. Check to see if it is right.

Here are the steps you follow with every list.

Test	Test a new list.
Mark	Mark the test.
Notebook	Put learning words in your notebook.
Hardspots	Underline your **hardspots**.
Learning	Learn your words.
Activities	Work from this book.
Learning	Learn your words again.
Retest	Test the list again.
Score	Colour in your graph. (In the Teacher's Guide.)
Tough Ones	Mistakes go in this list.

Reviews and Tough Ones

Other Words

Your teacher will give you words from your other school work to learn, and there may be some words from your own writing. Put these in your notebook and learn them as well.

I'll let you know when a Review or Tough Ones test is coming. These tests are important. They help you to retain the spellings you have learned.

Activity Words

At the end of each exercise in this book check all your spelling. Put your error words in the next week's list.

The Glossary

Use the glossary on page 48 to help you to work through the activities in this book. It will help you to learn the technical terms of word study.

Technology

Learn to use technology to work with words. Ask your teacher to show you how to use a thesaurus, and find out how you can make use of an electronic spellchecker.

Build up your WORD POWER!

Unit 1

List 1

absolutely	announcement	automobile	cannibal
colourful	creak	democratic	ecstasy
expression	funeral	impatient	management
muscles	pause	preparation	rehearse
signature	stadium	superior	training

List 2

abundance	annual	awfully	canvas
column	creature	deny	efficiency
extend	furious	include	manoeuvre
musician	peaceful	prepared	reliable
similar	stalk	supermarket	trampoline

List 3

accept	anonymous	awkward	capacity
combine	cricket	deposit	efficient
extension	furry	inconvenient	manuka
mysteries	pearl	preparing	remainder
siren	stallion	supplies	transferred

List 4

accidentally	Antarctica	bachelor	capsule
commission	criticism	descending	elbow
extraordinary	gallop	indicate	marae
mysterious	peculiar	presence	remark
situated	stare	surgeon	travelling

List 5

accommodate	anxiously	bacteria	carefully
companion	criticise	descent	element
facsimile	gem	individual	marriage
navigation	penguin	preserve	remembrance
situation	staring	surrender	tremble

Unit 1 — List 1 Exercises

1 Complete this table:

Verb	Noun
announce	announcement
manage	management
adjust	
	detachment
govern	

2 Write some extensions of the **root word** of expression using the **suffixes** ' –ed', '–ing', '–ive', '–less', '–ible' and '–ly'. (You may have to use two together.) We found six.

3 Find list words that are **synonyms** for:
   better   eager   arena   rest

4 Find all the words beginning with the letter 'a' in Lists 1 to 5 and write them in alphabetical order.

5 Make a list of all the **nouns** beginning with the letters 'e' and 'f' in Lists 1 to 5.

6 Which list word has a **prefix** that creates an **antonym**?

Take a **root** word…

…add a **prefix** in front of it…

…add a **suffix** after it and you get an extension.

Unit 1 — List 2 Exercises

1. Write the **root word** of reliable. Now add **prefixes** and **suffixes** to build as many extensions as you can. (We found nine.)

2. Now write the **root words** of all the other extensions in List 2.

3. Which list words are **synonyms** for:
   yearly   angry   trustworthy   stretch   pillar

4. Which list words answer these clues?
   Tent fabric.   Thrilling bouncer.
   Tuneful player.   More than enough.
   Tall support with a silent 'n'.

5. Find the missing **vowels** and write the list words.
   prprd   crtr   pcfl   mscn   bndnc

6. Write the single-**syllable** word in List 2.

Technology option
Use a spellchecker to find words with the **suffix** '–ive'.
Code in ?????ive. Press ENTER.
Now try ??????ive and ???????ive.

Hurry up, Nic. We've got swimming next.

I *am* hurrying but there's so much to do.

Unit 1

List 3 Exercises

1. Write these list words as separate **syllables**:
   inconvenient   awkward   manuka   capacity

2. Complete this table:

Extension	Root	Suffix
supplies		
mysteries		
extension		
	accept	–ance
	deposit	–or

3. Which list words mean almost the same as:
   Moved to another place.   Mix with.
   Left over.   Nameless.

4. Put Jem's list words right. Underline the **hardspots**.

   anonimous prepering transfered perl capasity

5. Fill the puzzle grid with list words.

6. Review Lists 33, 34 and 35 of Book 7.

You're a pain!

Make it a habit
Always check all your spelling in these activities.

Unit 1 — List 4 Exercises

1. Find all the **nouns** in List 4. Write the **proper noun f**irst.
2. Write the two list words that name types of people.
3. Fill the gaps with list words.
   The _____ made an incision with the scalpel.
   The _____ contained a dangerous drug.
   There was no _____ of his conduct.
   The declaration was made in the _____ of a magistrate.

4. Add the missing punctuation marks and capital letters.

   oh said nicola i cant possibly learn all these words

5. Write the plural form of:
   bachelor   criticism   marae   peculiarity

6. Unscramble these list words:
   cendgidens   learntivlg   hbcraole   ustadtie   pearluci

Singular

Plural

Unit 1 — List 5 Exercises

1 Complete the table:

Verb	Noun
_____er	remembrance
accommodate	_____tion
preserve	_____tion
	navigation
_____y	marriage

2 Build other words with this unusual ending: bacter**ia**
caf _ _ _ _ ia   mal _ _ ia   pet _ _ ia
hys _ _ _ ia   ins _ _ _ ia   sub _ _ _ ia

3 Replace the underlined words with a list word.
The <u>fax</u> arrived before lunch.
The <u>germs</u> multiplied rapidly.
The cabin could <u>hold</u> six passengers.
Every <u>person</u> must be searched.

4 Put these list words right. Underline the **hardspots**.
acomodate   facsmile   individial
stareing   rememberance

5 Can you think of some words that start like this one: <u>sw</u>ay?
exhange: sw_____
fork-tailed bird: sw_____
to cheat someone: sw_____
make an oath: sw_____
water circulation: sw_____

6 Use the Codebreaker on page 48 to work out this message:
OGK'T UMECSTBWG MNWBEBWBGJ MTG ZKD TMNBPL MPA VBJWGPBPL WC KSJBN.

INTER-SCHOOL SWIMMING TEAM

Boys
James
Bobby
Jem
Ben

Girls
Awhina
Nicola
Annie
Jane

Practices in the pool 12:30pm daily.

Unit 2

List 6

accommodation	appeal	badge	cassette
comparatively	crocodile	describe	embarrass
faith	generally	industries	martyr
necessarily	perform	president	repetition
skateboard	starve	survive	tremendous

List 7

accompanied	appetite	banner	catalogue
compare	cuddle	description	embarrassment
faithful	genius	industrious	marvellous
necessity	personal	previous	represent
skeleton	starving	suspicious	trial

List 8

accompany	apply	banquet	catastrophe
compass	cultivate	deserve	emergency
false	Germany	influence	massive
nevertheless	personally	pride	representative
skilful	steady	swallow	troop

List 9

according	applying	barbecue	catches
compel	cordially	desire	encourage
familiar	gigantic	initial	matinee
nickel	perspiration	prisoner	reserve
slammed	steak	swamp	tropical

List 10

accurate	appoint	bargain	caterpillar	competition
correspondence	desperate	encyclopedia*	fantastic	giraffe
innocent	mechanical	noble	persuade	privilege
reservoir	smelt	stereo	sway	turtle

* The form 'encyclopaedia' is also correct. We have chosen 'encyclopedia' according to the Concise Oxford Dictionary (Tenth edition).

Unit 2

List 6 Exercises

1 Complete this table:

2 Write the **compound word** in List 6 as two **nouns**. The second part of the word **noun** occurs in many other words. Can you think of some?
cup_____
key_____
over_____

Singular	Plural
badge	
	industries
martyr	

3 Which list words are **synonyms** for:
trust   act   plead   relate

4 Write all the single-**syllable** words in List 6.

5 List all the reptiles in Lists 6 to 10.

6

Review Lists 1, 2 and 3 plus any Tough Ones.

You just make life difficult!

An interesting homework task
Make a list of all the **synonyms** for big. Use a thesaurus or spellchecker to help you. Display your list on the classroom wall.

Unit 2 — List 7 Exercises

1. Apply the **noun** test to find all the naming words in List 7.

2. What is the **root word** of faithful? Now add **prefixes** and **suffixes** to build as many extensions as you can. (We found five.)

3. Which list words are synonyms for:
   list   loyal
   streamer   talent
   diligent

4. Which list words answer these clues?
   Not the one after.
   We meant to make you blush.
   Could be a list of felines.
   Scary frame.
   Long time empty tummy.

5. Can you work out these skeletal bones?
   s _ _ _ l   s _ _ n _
   _ em _ r   _ i _
   _ _ ou _ _ e _

6. Use one **prefix** to turn accompanied and faithful into their **antonyms**.

Marvellous - industrious - faithful - genius... hmm, this list describes me so well!

Training time for fast finishers

The puzzles grids on pages 7, 13, 19 and so on, and so on are not hard to make. Try making your own with the words in this list.

Unit 2

List 8 Exercises

1. Write the **root words** of:
   skilful   personally   accompany   emergency

2. Write the one-, two- and three-**syllable** words in this list.

3. Which list words mean almost the same as:
   Total disaster.   Unusually large.
   Go with.   Send your application to.

4. Put these list words right.
   Underline the **hardspots**.
   personly   skillful
   bancquet   acompny
   catastrophy

5. German people come from Germany.
   What do you call people who come from:
   Wellington   Wales
   The Netherlands   Mexico   Bali

6. Fill the puzzle grid with list words.

> If you are getting too many words in your Tough Ones list you may not be learning your words efficiently. Go back to page 1 to check your learning strategy.

Unit 2 — List 9 Exercises

1. Write these list words in **syllables**:
   barbecue   compel   gigantic
   tropical   prisoner   catches

2. Complete this table:

Verb	Noun
_____ire	perspiration
encourage	_____ment
reserve	_____tion
im_____	prisoner

   You can use a spellchecker to solve Exercise 5. Look on page 6 for help.

3. Fill the gaps with list words.
   We went to the _____ performance at 2pm.
   _____ trickled down her back.
   We were greeted _____ at the door.
   I can't _____ you to take on this mission.

4. Add the missing punctuation marks and capital letters.
   nicola said that we shouldnt miss her bands concert

5. Nickel is a metal. Can you think of some others?
   l _ _ d   _ op _ _ _
   _ _ um _ _ i _ _   _ r _ _
   _ i _ c

   I suppose we have to take this rodent creature seriously.

6. Review Lists 4, 5 and 6.

   'fraid so.

Unit 2 — List 10 Exercises

1. Find the missing letters and write the list words:
   _ _ r _ _ i _   _ _ _ er _ _ l _ _ _
   _ o _ _ _ _ it _ _ _   _ u _ t _ _
   _ _ _ a _ _ e

   What do you notice about these words?

2. Make a list of all the words in List 10 that have *more than* three **syllables**.

3. Replace the underlined words with **synonyms** from List 10:
   Their arguments will <u>convince</u> you.
   These suggestions are <u>amazing</u>.
   Marie entered the <u>contest</u>.
   The judge said that he was <u>not guilty</u>.

   > corispondance
   > privelege
   > apoint
   > catterpiller

4. Put these list words right. Underline the **hardspots**.

5. Use the Codebreaker on page 48 to work out this message:
   WYG JWSAGPWJ TGMVVI VBFG WC VBJWGP WC PBNCVM'J ZMPA.

6. *Technology option*

   Sometimes American spelling and English spelling differ. For example: color (A) colour (E). Work together to find other examples. Display your discoveries on the classroom wall. An American spellchecker or dictionary could help you.

Unit 3

List 11

acknowledge	appointment	battery	cease
competitor	courageous	dessert	endeavour
fascinated	grammar	inquire	memories
numerous	physical	proceed	responsibility
snatched	stew	sweat	trying

List 12

acknowledgement	appreciated	beautifully	celebration
complain	courteous	determined	engage
fashion	glory	insist	memorable
nursery	physician	procedure	resources
sneak	sticky	sweater	undoubtedly

List 13

acquaintance	approach	beggar	cemetery
complexion	courtesy	devote	enormous
fatigue	grocery	instant	mention
obedience	pickle	profit	revolver
sneezed	stitch	switch	unforgettable

List 14

acrobatic	appropriate	believing	centennial
composition	crackers	diameter	enthusiasm
fault	guarantee	interfere	mere
obedient	picnicking	prominent	revolution
society	stolen	syllable	unnecessary

List 15

adjective	approval	benefit	ceremony
concerned	crane	difficulty	entrance
favourable	guardian	intermediate	merely
observe	pledge	pronunciation	rhyme
softball	storey	sympathy	urge

Unit 3 — List 11 Exercises

1. Write the **plural** form of:
   battery　　　　dessert　　　　stew

   Which List 11 word is a **plural**? Write its **singular** form.

2. Write any two-**syllable nouns** in List 11.

3. Write list words that are **synonyms** for:
   fearless　　many　　enchanted　　engagement

4. Which list words are **antonyms** of:
   few　　　　commence　　　　halt
   cowardly　　dismiss

5. Nine words ending with 'y' in Lists 11 to 15 have **root words**. Write the **root words**.

6. This coded message has had all the vowels removed. What does it say?

   W d'nt thnk tht Ncl lks th Rvw rmndr rdnt.

   I bet that wretched rodent is on the very next page.

Unit 3 — List 12 Exercises

1. Complete this table:

List word	Root word	Prefix	Suffix(es)
acknowledgement			
undoubtedly			
celebration		—	
beautifully		—	

2. With a little modification you can add the **suffix** '–ure' to the word 'proceed' to make 'procedure'. Add the same **suffix** to:

   create   expose   moist
   please   press

3. Which list words are **synonyms** for:

   trend   demand   doctor
   moan   polite

4. Which list words answer these clues?
   A little kid's den.
   Go on, nag about it!
   Could be a pullover OR a runner on a hot day.
   Toffee that's not quite set.
   Birthday party for a naughty child.

5. Write these **synonyms** for sneak. You can use a spellchecker or thesaurus to work them out.

   _ ku _ _   _ u _ k   c _ _ e _

6. Review Lists 7, 8, and 9 plus any Tough Ones.

Unit 3 — List 13 Exercises

1. Use **prefixes** to make the **antonyms** of:
   courtesy   obedience

   Which list word has a **prefix** making it an **antonym**?

2. Write the **plural** form of:
   courtesy   beggar   cemetery
   grocery   switch

3. Which list words have almost the same meaning as:
   Come close to.   Proceeds from trading.
   Ready cooked.   Very memorable.

4. Put Nicola's list words right.
   Underline the **hardspots**.

   complection
   sneesed
   certesy enormiss
   fatiuge

5. Pickles are found in the pantry.
   What other pantry items come in jars or bottles?
   s _ _ c _   _ _ m
   _ ay _ n _ a _ _ _   _ r _ s _ _ n _

6. Fill the puzzle grid with list words.

Good advice

Even an expert speller uses a dictionary to check on rarely used words.

Unit 3

List 14 Exercises

1. Complete this table:

Verb	Noun
_____se	composition
picnicking	
_____se	enthusiasm
interfere	_____nce

2. Unscramble these list words:
   mintropne
   patporreapi
   tenodebi
   loonvutier

3. Fill the gaps with list words.
   Because the appliance had been _____, the _____ could not demand to have the _____ repaired under the _____ .

4. Add the missing punctuation marks and capital letters.

   will you be going to tonights show asked freda

5. Crackers are a type of biscuit. Can you think of some others?
   s _ _ r _ b _ _ a _
   _ ho _ _ l _ _ _
   S _ _ _ w _ b _ r _
   _ af _ _

6. Write the **root words** of:
   believing
   composition
   picnicking
   revolution

But Nic, even acrobats have to learn their spelling.

Unit 3

List 15 Exercises

1. You can add the **suffix** '–able' to 'favour' to make 'favourable'. Now add the same **suffix** to these words:
   adapt admire
   debate honour
   comfort

2. Apply your **noun** test to identify all the **nouns** in List 15.

3. Replace the underlined words with a list word.
   The new office was on the fifth <u>floor</u>.
   The money was of little <u>use</u> to the old people.
   We needed the local council's <u>blessing</u> before going ahead.
   I wasn't criticising, I was <u>just</u> pointing out your error.

4. Put these list words right. Underline the **hardspots**.
   benifit   pronounceation   gardian
   ryhme   faverable

5. Use the Codebreaker on page 48 to work out this message:
   YCQ AC ICS FPCQ BU WYGTG BJ M JXGVVBPL KBJWMFG BP M ABNWBCPMTI?

6. Review Lists 10, 11 and 12.

No, Nicola… a broken leg does not get you off spelling class.

At last I get a rest from Nicola. She fell off her swing!

Unit 4

List 16
admission	approximately	bluff	certainty
conductor	crashes	dinghy	equally
feature	guerilla	interrupt	messenger
occurred	pneumonia	propeller	rhythm
solar	stormy	symphony	useless

List 17
advance	apricot	bossy	certificate
conference	crayfish	directly	equipped
ferocious	guitar	introduce	microphone
occurrence	poisonous	proportion	risk
solo	straighten	tablet	vain

List 18
advertise	aquarium	boulder	chamber
confidence	curiosity	disagreeable	errand
fiery	gymnasium	introduction	microscope
official	policy	propose	sacrifice
solution	stranded	tariff	vary

List 19
advertisement	arose	bounce	championship
confident	curious	disappointment	error
filthy	hamburger	invalid	minimum
opinion	polished	prosperous	satisfactorily
solve	strategy	task	varying

List 20
advise	arrangement	branches	changeable
conjunction	curve	disaster	establish
financial	handsome	investigate	mischievous
opportunity	pollution	punish	satisfactory
somersault	strawberry	telescope	vast

Unit 4

List 16 Exercises

1. Write in **syllables** any list words where the letter 'y' is acting as a vowel.

2. Write the **root words** of:
   admission   certainty   conductor
   equally   messenger   occurred

3. Which list words are **synonyms** for:
   courier   windy
   characteristic   assurance

4. Make a list of all the **nouns** beginning with the letter 'a' in Lists 16 to 20.

5. Many words in Lists 16 to 20 begin with the letter 's'. Convert as many of them as you can into their **plural** forms.

6. You looked at American and English spelling on page 15. Compare words ending with '–ize' and '–ise'. A spellchecker could help. What major difference did you find?

24
Spelling in the lives of Jem and Nicola

Draw your own picture of everyday life. Put the headings around the edge and under each heading write your list of words.

Check your spelling carefully.

Display your project on the wall.

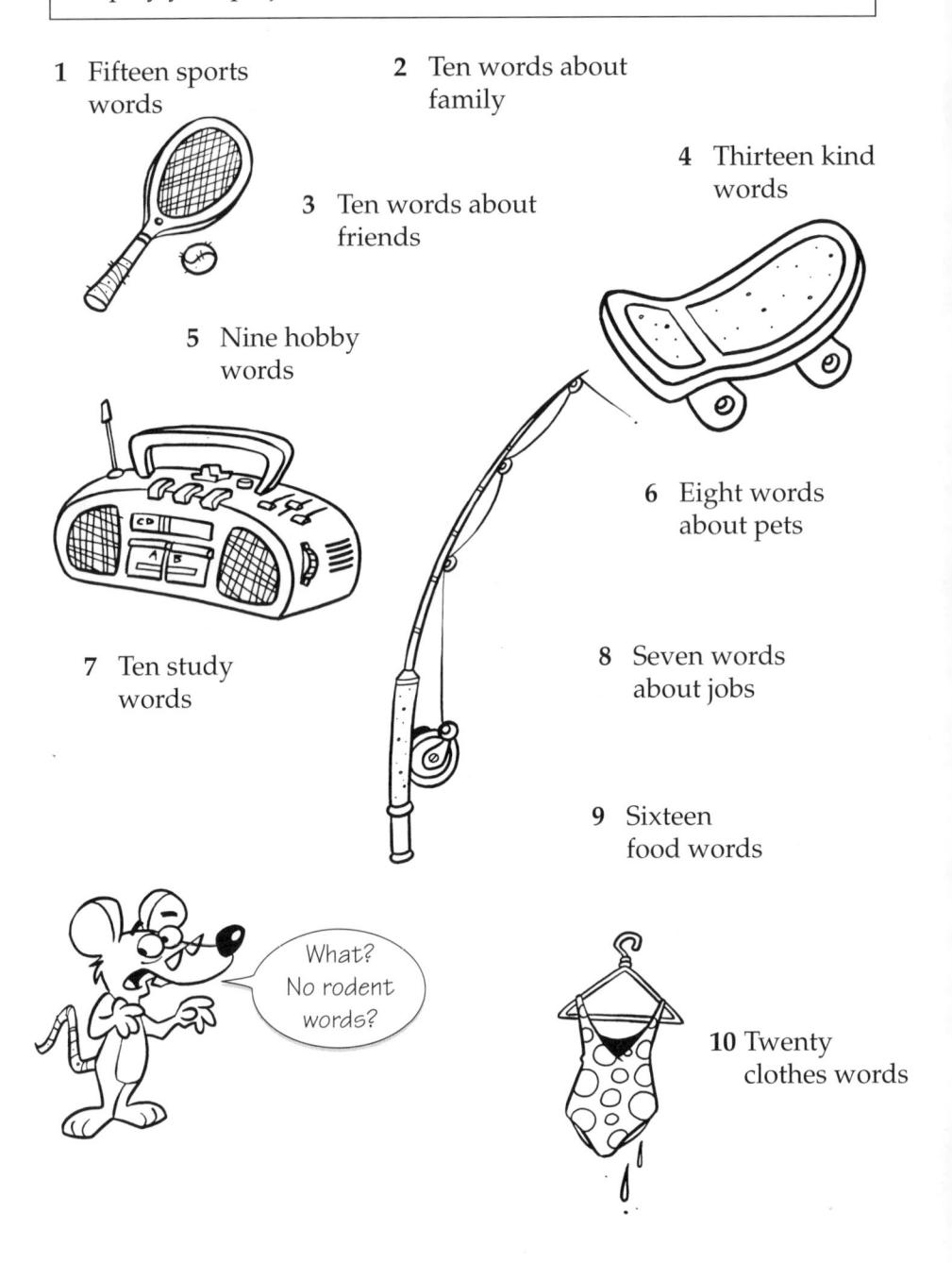

1 Fifteen sports words

2 Ten words about family

3 Ten words about friends

4 Thirteen kind words

5 Nine hobby words

6 Eight words about pets

7 Ten study words

8 Seven words about jobs

9 Sixteen food words

What? No rodent words?

10 Twenty clothes words

25

11 Eleven words about school

12 Fourteen entertainment words

13 Twelve music words

14 Eighteen technological words

15 Eight modern teenage words

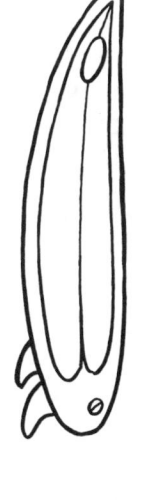

Unit 4

List 17 Exercises

1. Which two list words have the **suffix** '–ence'?

   Now add the same **suffix** to extend these words: (Watch out for spelling traps.)

   | emerge | impudent | obedient |
   | prefer | subside | turbulent |

2. Write these list words in **syllables**:

   | certificate | proportion | introduce |
   | microphone | conference | |

3. Which list words are synonyms for:

   | award | share | pill |
   | conceited | autocratic | |

4. Which list words answer these clues?

   Peachy colour. Very angry animal.
   Small voice conductor. A happening wasteful with 'c's and 'r's.
   This one isn't a blood transporter.

5. A guitar is a musical instrument. Here are some more instruments without their **vowels**. What are they?

   | clrnt | vln | sxphn |
   | trmpt | | |

6. Write the letters 'a e i o u' in ascending order according to the number of times they occur in List 17.

Unit 4

List 18 Exercises

1. Complete this table:

Verb	Noun
_____ce	introduction
propose	_____tion
vary	____tion

2. Write the **homonym** of boulder. Now use both words to fill the gaps.
   The crane lifted the massive _____.
   David was _____ than Goliath.

3. Which list words mean almost the same as:
   Give up.   Left behind.
   Quick tempered.   Fish tank.

4. Put these list words right. Underline the **hardspots**.
   erand   gimnasium   sacrefice
   disagreable   acquarium

5. Fill the puzzle grid with list words.

What are you so annoyed about?

I'm only halfway through my spelling project and that THING!!?? wants me to do a review!

6. Review Lists 13, 14 and 15 plus any Tough Ones.

Unit 4

List 19 Exercises

1 Fill the gaps with list words.
   The team was _____ that it would win.
   You must develop a _____ to _____ the problem.
   The _____ for the car had an _____ in the text.

2 Add the missing punctuation marks and capital letters.

   i wish wed less work to do in these books announced bill

3 Unscramble these list words:
   usicrou   dilphose   vaindil
   manhopchisip   frocstyasati

4 Some words are shortened when we use them in speech. What short versions would you use for:
   advertisement   champion   hamburger

5 The same list word could be used to fill both these gaps. Write the word.
   The _____ cast a vote that was _____ .

6 Reorganise these **syllables** to make five list words:
   i – fact – i – ment – on – con – or – cham – fi – point – mum – ship – is – ap – pi – sat – dis – ly – dent – min

Are you my opposite?

No. I'm your inverse.

Unit 4

List 20 Exercises

1 Unscramble these list words:
   bistalshe   harbnesc   noltluipo   sisterad

2 What are the **root words** of:
   arrangement   changeable   financial
   satisfactory   pollution

3 Replace the underlined words with a list word.
   The flood was a <u>catastrophe</u>.
   He was a very <u>good-looking</u> man.
   The <u>piece</u> he had written for three violins was particularly beautiful.
   She decided to <u>found</u> an organisation to save the penguin.

4 Put these list words right. Underline the **hardspots**.
   summersalt   opertunity   mischivous
   cerve   changable

5 Work out these **synonyms** for vast:
   _ n _ r _ o _ s   _ _ g _
   _ ig _ _ _ _ c   _ ol _ _ s _ _

6 Use the Codebreaker on page 48 to work out this message:
   YMEG ICS GEGT UCSPA M QCTA WYMW ABAP'W YMEG M ECQGV?

I hope you've finished your spelling projects.

I'm up to date at last.

Me too! Now let's start practicing for another concert.

Unit 5

List 21

aerial	artificial	breathing	charm
conqueror	cycle	discipline	eventually
flavour	hangi	invisible	miserable
optimistic	portion	purchase	sauna
soul	stretch	television	vegetation

List 22

affair	ascend	brief	chauffeur
conscience	cylinder	discussion	evidence
foal	happiest	irresistible	missionary
ordinarily	possess	quantities	scarcely
source	struggle	temper	vengeance

List 23

affect	assistance	brilliant	chemist
conscious	debt	disguise	exaggerate
foggy	heavier	Italian	misspelled
ore	possession	questionnaire	schedule
souvenir	stumble	temperament	vicinity

List 24

affectionately	assistant	Britain	chemistry
consent	deceive	dissatisfied	examine
footsteps	helicopter	justify	modelling
organisation	possibility	quilt	scrubbing
spaceship	stupid	temporary	victory

List 25

agent	associate	chopped	considerably
decision	distinct	exclaim	forecast
herald	laboratory	monotonous	original
pounce	radish	saxophone	secure
sparkle	submarine	territory	vigorous

Unit 5

List 21 Exercises

1 Make a list of all the two-**syllable nouns** in List 21.

2 Write the **antonym** of invisible? Now add the **suffix** '–ity'.

3 Which list words are **synonyms** for:
   taste   synthetic
   punish   extend

4 Make a list of the words in Lists 21 to 25 that have two sets of double letters.

5 Replace the **vowels** lost from these list words:
   nvsbl   dscpln
   ptmstc   vntll
   tlvsn

6 Review Lists 16, 17 and 18.

Can we please do our band practice now, Mr D?

Not until you've done your review test.

Oh bother!

Unit 5

List 22 Exercises

1. The **prefix** 'ir–' changes a word to its **antonym**. Add it to:
   responsible   repairable
   regular   reverent

2. Write the **homonym** of source. Now use both words to fill the gaps.
   "Please pass the _____ ."
   "What is the _____ of your information?"

3. Which list words are **synonyms** for:
   strive   own   driver   proof   climb

4. Which list words answer these clues?
   Religious worker.
   Under normal circumstances.
   Oral interaction.
   You wouldn't put this one on a hamburger.
   Try hard to overcome all those 'g's.

5. Foal/mare. Fill the gaps with other child/parent pairs.
   _____ /duck   _____ /cat
   _____ /goose   _____ /sow
   _____ /giraffe

6. Write the letters 'a e i o u' in ascending order according to the number of times they occur in List 22.

Unit 5 — List 23 Exercises

1. What is the first **syllable** in the word **conscious**?

   Now add it to these endings to make five new words:
   - –tract
   - –cussion
   - –flict
   - –dition
   - –cern

   No reviews, no Tough Ones, no projects. Guess what I'm thinking?

   Hockey practice?!

2. Write these list words in **syllables**:
   - possession
   - temperament
   - assistance
   - exaggerate

3. Which list words mean almost the same as:
   - Money owed.
   - Wide awake.
   - List of intended events.
   - Mineral-bearing rock.

4. Put these list words right. Underline the **hardspots**.
   - posession
   - visinity
   - briliant
   - victery
   - mispeled

5. Fill the puzzle grid with list words.

6. A **chemist** is a person who works with chemicals. How many other words in Lists 21 to 25 could be used to describe a person?

Unit 5 — List 24 Exercises

1. Make a list of all the **nouns** in List 24. Which one is a **proper noun**?

2. What is the **antonym** of dissatisfied?
   What is the **root word**?

3. Fill the gaps with list words.
   Is there any _____ of the _____ finding more members?
   It was _____ to think that I could _____ you.

4. Add the missing punctuation marks and capital letters.

   the last of mikes pencils are on the table next to that girls ruler

5. Chemistry is a science. Can you think of some others?
   b _ _ _ ny   bi _ _ _ gy
   ph _ _ _ _ s   z _ _ _ ogy
   ae _ on _ _ tics   as _ _ _ _ _ my
   ge _ _ _ _ y

6. Put those sticks down. It's time to review Lists 19, 20 and 21 plus Tough Ones.

   Take no notice of him...

   Suddenly I've gone quite deaf!

Unit 5

List 25 Exercises

1. Write the **plural** form of:
   radish   laboratory   agent
   associate   territory

2. Add **prefixes** to form the **antonyms** of:
   chopped   decision   distinct
   original   secure

3. Replace the underlined words with a list word.
   Farming is the main occupation in this <u>area</u>.
   She spoke in a very <u>boring</u> way.
   This one is <u>significantly</u> larger.
   What made you <u>connect</u> this event with the crime?

4. Put Nicola's list words right.
   Underline the **hardspots**.

   asosiate vigerous terittory sparckle decission

5. Use the Codebreaker on page 48 to work out this message:
   PBNCVM BJCSTJQ BKKBPL
   NYMKXB CP. JYGB JMTGMV
   VILCCA MWYVGW GWCC.

6. *More training for fast finishers*
   Try to make a puzzle grid for List 25. How many words can you fit into it?

Unit 6

List 26

agreeable	assume	bruise	Christian
constitution	declaration	distinguish	excursion
forehead	heroes	librarian	monotony
originally	practical	rattle	seize
specimen	substance	theory	villain

List 27

aisle	assure	bulletin	circumstance
construction	declare	distributed	exhausted
foreigner	hinge	likelihood	moral
otherwise	practically	recite	sensible
spectators	subtle	thorough	volcanoes

List 28

alcohol	astonished	bureau	civilisation
container	decoration	dolphin	exhibition
forfeit	hire	likely	mortgage
pace	praise	recommend	separation
spotted	suddenly	thoroughly	volunteer

List 29

alphabet	athlete	burrow	claim
content	defeat	doubt	exist
forgetful	hostage	liquor	mosquito
Pacific	preach	reduce	sergeant
sprang	sufficient	threaten	weird

List 30

altitude	athletics	cafeteria	cleanliness
continually	defence	doubtful	existence
former	homesick	literature	motel
parachute	precede	reference	series
sprinkle	suggestion	thrilled	whitebait

Unit 6 — List 26 Exercises

1. Write the **compound word** in List 26 as two words. Now add the second part of the word to these beginnings to make six new **compound words**:
   bridge–   mast–   bed–
   over–   arrow–   block–

2. Use **prefixes** and **suffixes** to build extensions of the **root word** assume. How many can you make? (We found seven.)

3. Which list words are **synonyms** for:
   rogue   damage
   idea   outing

   Urgently needed for List 27: one mouse trap to rid this book of rodents!

4. Which list words answer these clues:
   Book worker.
   Out and about.
   We're happy with lots of 'e's.
   In the beginning.
   You can clearly see it's got three eyes.

5. Unscramble these list words:
   brainiarl   cracalpit   busecnast
   micesnep   cadearntiol

6. If you change two **consonants** in a list word you turn boredom into a famous board game. Write the list word and the name of the game.

More good advice

Start using word puzzle books. They keep your vocabulary growing.

Unit 6

List 27 Exercises

1 Three words associated with weddings – aisle, altar, and hymn – all have **homonyms**. Write the h**omonyms** in order to find out what the bride said about the bride groom.

2 Complete this table:

Verb	Noun
recite	_____tion
declare	_____tion
	construction
assure	_____nce

3 Which list words are **synonyms** for:
report   complete   onlookers
building   corridor

4 Which list words answer these clues?
Fire-spouting rock chuckers.
We had to ask Clare to leave.
Bill's a really smart kid.
Not really a gunshot wound.
Potatoes wearing glasses.

5 Write all the single-**syllable** words in List 27.

6 Review Lists 22, 23 and 24.

You just never give up, do you? Maybe I should get a rodent-eating cat?

Look in the glossary on the inside back cover. Cover the explanations. How many terms do you understand now?

Unit 6

List 28 Exercises

1. The **suffix** '–eer' indicates 'a person'.
   Use this **suffix** to name:
   a person who climbs mountains
   a person who works with engines
   a person who runs an auction
   a person who takes part in a mutiny

2. Find all the two-**syllable nouns** in List 28.

3. Which list words mean almost the same as:
   House loan.   Information centre.
   Give up.   Public display.

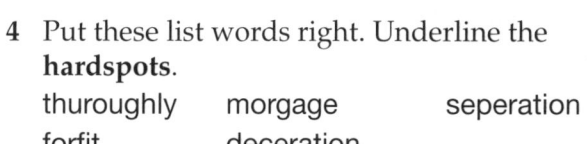

4. Put these list words right. Underline the **hardspots**.
   thuroughly   morgage   seperation
   forfit   deceration

5. Can you work out these ancient civilisations?
   _ gy _ _ _ _ n   _ r _ e _   _ _ m _ n
   B _ z _ n _ _ _ _   _ z _ _ _

6. Fill the puzzle grid with list words.

That rodent has helped me keep my Tough Ones list down to just 4!

Yeah… he's a nuisance, but I guess he does help…

Nicola and Jem are beginning to get the picture – at last!

Unit 6

List 29 Exercises

1. The **suffix** '–ful' adds the meaning 'full of' to a word. Write the word that means:
   full of mercy   full of wonder
   full of dread   full of grace

2. Go back through Lists 1 to 29 to find all the **proper nouns** we have met so far in this book.

3. Fill the gaps with list words.
   The guerillas took a _____ from the group of tourists.
   Is there _____ milk in the jug?
   We were _____ to spend the night in the hut.
   A _____-looking man approached us.

4. Add the missing punctuation marks and capital letters.

   for miris fruit salad we need some apples grapes and peaches

5. The mosquito is a type of insect. Can you think of some others?
   b _ _ _ l _   s _ _ _ f _ _
   dr _ _ _ _ _ _ _   _ e _ a

6. Find the eighth and ninth words from Lists 26 to 30 and write them in alphabetical order.

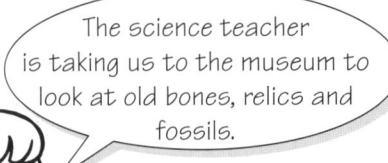

   The science teacher is taking us to the museum to look at old bones, relics and fossils.

   Do you think we'll see anyone we know?

Unit 6 — List 30 Exercises

1. Write any list words that are *not* **nouns**.

2. Write the three-**syllable** words in List 30.

3. Replace the underlined words with a list word.
   The <u>diner</u>, which was known for its <u>spotlessness</u>, had <u>fish</u> on the menu.
   During our stay at the <u>inn</u> I was <u>constantly</u> <u>depressed</u>.

4. Put these list words right. Underline the **hardspots**.
   continuly   parashute   preceed
   refrence   litrature

5. Use the Codebreaker on page 48 to work out this message:
   OGT GKI' JVG MTP GAW CJX GVV MGT CPM SWB NMV. PCQ YGQ MPW JWC ZGM PMB TVB PGX BVCW.

6. Review Lists 25, 26 and 27 plus any Tough Ones.

Unit 7

List 31
amateur	Atlantic	campaign	closely
convenience	definitely	dutiful	expedition
formula	humorous	locate	mould
parallel	precious	referred	severe
squash	suitability	tickled	worthy

List 32
amazement	attach	canal	clump
conversation	delicate	earnest	expense
fortunate	icicle	loneliness	moveable
parliament	prefer	refrigeration	shearing
squeak	suitable	tournament	worried

List 33
American	attachment	cancer	cobweb
co-operation	delight	earthquake	expensive
fragile	ignorance	losing	movement
particularly	preference	refugees	shrieking
squeeze	suitcase	trace	wrestle

List 34
analyse	attempt	candidate	coffin
copies	delightful	economic	experiment
freckles	imitation	make-up	mule
pastime	preferred	regretted	siege
squid	sunbathe	tragically	wrestling

List 35
anniversary	authority	candy	colonel
cordial	demand	economical	explanation
frequently	immigrants	magnificent	municipal
patient	prejudice	reign	signalled
squirt	superintendent	tragedy	wriggle

Unit 7

List 31 Exercises

1. Write the **root words** of:
   closely   definitely   dutiful
   humorous   referred   suitability

2. Write the list words that are **antonyms** of:
   distantly   lose   professional
   tragic   valueless

   Make a list of all the words you met at the museum last week.

   Groan.

3. Write the list words that are **synonyms** for:
   journey   valuable   stern
   handiness   reputable

4. Reorganise these **syllables** to make five list words:
   a – tion – ven – mu – i – i – it – or – la – suit – ence –
   for – bil – ex – con – ped – hum – y – ous

5. Use the same list word to fill both gaps.
   You'll have to _____ the clothes into the bag.
   Let's play _____.

6. Which list words answer these tricky clues?
   An ache when camping.
   Find Kate.
   Little bug that made you giggle.
   Scrambled verse plus 'e'.
   Three 'I's that never meet.

   I can only remember 'old' and 'fossil'.

Unit 7 — List 32 Exercises

1. Write these list words in **syllables**:
   conversation   refrigeration   amazement
   tournament   loneliness

2. Unscramble these list words:
   redrowi   pexense   rantese
   tideacle   busteali

3. Which list words are **synonyms** for:
   transferable   lucky   choose
   appropriate   fragile

4. Which list words answer these clues?
   Wool removal process.
   A house for official talking.
   Definitely not screwed to the floor.
   Usually indicates that oil is required but don't try to oil a mouse.
   Is this Kate who works in the delicatessen?

5. What is the **root word** of moveable? Now add **prefixes** and **suffixes** to make extensions. (We found nine.)

6. Make a coded message using the Codebreaker on page 48. Try it out on your friend.

Unit 7

List 33 Exercises

1 These list words have got mixed up with each other. Write the original words.
   suitquake   earthweb
   cobcase

   What kind of words are they?

2 How many four-**syllable nouns** are there in this list?

3 Which list words mean almost the same as:
   Breaks easily.   Lack of knowledge.
   Added part.   Homeless aliens.

4 Put these list words right. Underline the **hardspots**.
   coperation   atachment   particlarly
   preferance   reffugees

5 Fill the puzzle grid with list words.

6 Review Lists 28, 29 and 30.

Let's have one more concert before we finish Book 8.

What a celebration!

That's a great idea!

Unit 7

List 34 Exercises

1 Complete this table:

Verb	Noun
analyse	_____sis
	imitation
preferred	_____ence
wrestling	_____er

2 Make lists of the one- and two-**syllable** words in List 34.

3 Fill the gaps with list words.
The _____ had to _____ the _____ to pass the science examination.
His favourite _____ was _____.

4 Add the missing punctuation marks and capital letters.
no i need six boys boots said the coach dont you understand plain english

5 Can you work out these **synonyms** for imitation? A spellchecker or thesaurus could help you.
m _ _ k   s _ _ m
c _ _ y   s _ _ st _ _ _ t _
a _ _ _ f _ _ i _ l

6 Unscramble these list words:
comiconeal   otinamiti   tubhasen
fredreper   tiemaps

Unit 7

List 35 Exercises

1. What are the **root words** of:
   economical frequently
   explanation signalled

2. Write the **hononym** of reign. Which of the two words means precipitation?

3. Replace the underlined words with a list word.
   He may <u>influence</u> the others.
   Clothed in snow, the mountain was a <u>majestic</u> sight.
   The loss of her husband was a terrible <u>misfortune</u>.
   What was their <u>case</u> for going there?

4. Put these list words right. Underline the **hardspots**.
   aniversary pregudice
   imigrents tradgedy
   ecconomical

5. Use the Codebreaker on page 48 to work out this message:
   ICSYMEG NCKXVGW GAZCCFGB LYW. NCPL TMWSVMW BCPJ!

6. Review Lists 31 and 32 plus any Tough Ones.

   Not quite, Nicola. You should try my other book — Now You Can Spell.

   This is the end!

   Made it at last!

> Here is your Codebreaker.
> The top letter is the code.
> The bottom letter
> is the message.

Codebreaker

The top letter is the code. The bottom letter is the message.

A	B	C	D	E	F	G	H	I	J	K	L	M
D	I	O	X	V	K	E	Q	Y	S	M	G	A

N	O	P	Q	R	S	T	U	V	W	X	Y	Z
C	J	N	W	Z	U	R	F	L	T	P	H	B

Glossary

antonym: word that is opposite in meaning to another word.
compound word: word made of two words e.g. handrail.
consonant: all the letters except a e i o u and sometimes y.
extension: word made by adding a prefix and/or suffix to a root word e.g. break (r.w.): unbreakable.
homonym: word with similar pronunciation but with a different spelling e.g. there: their.
noun: word that names something e.g. Peter, clock, love.
plural: word denoting more than one e.g. books, hooves, babies, boys'.
prefix: common first syllable added to a root word e.g. untie, prewar.
proper noun: naming word that starts with a capital letter e.g. Mary, Mr Jones, Brighton, River Dee.
punctuation: full stops, commas, speech marks, apostrophes, etc.
root word: word capable of being extended with a prefix and/or a suffix e.g. accept (r.w.): unacceptable.
singular: word denoting only one of something e.g. book, baby, boy's.
suffixes: one or more commonly used syllables added after a root word e.g. spare (r.w.) sparingly.
syllable: word segment containing a vowel sound e.g. un-dig-nif-ied.
synonym: word having almost the same meaning e.g. big, hug, large.
verb: word meaning an action or state e.g. jump, is, was, arrive, move, etc.
vowel: a e i o u and sometimes y.